BE AMAZING!

A 10-step guide to achieving your career goals.

LUIS EDUARDO DEL RIO AZCONA

LUIS EDUARDO DEL RIO AZCONA

Born in Guadalajara, Jalisco, México. Started his professional career in 1994 just before graduating from college (Business administration- UNIVA).

He has held human resources leadership positions at major international technology corporations, leading projects across the Americas & Europe.

Complementing his experience with post degrees about Business and People Management: (ITAM- México, INALDE- Colombia, Harvard- U.S. & Munich University- Germany).

Husband, father, consultant, entrepreneur, professor at the university, speaker, and passionate about people´s development, coaching, health, music, cars, coffee, and tennis.

BE AMAZING!
A 10-step guide to achieving your career goals.

A practical and inspiring guide to unlock your potential and thrive on your professional career.

It provides a clear and comprehensive framework for identifying your strengths and weaknesses, setting goals, action plans, and keep growing.

By following the 10 steps in this book, you will unlock your professional possibilities and achieve your career goals, just like magic!

Who said there is no formula for success?

After years of research, *BE AMAZING!* is giving the key, full of examples and exercises to outline your dreams.

If you are focus on developing the best version of you... *BE AMAZING!* is what you are looking for.

BE AMAZING!
A 10-step guide to achieving your career goals.

Dedicated to all people aiming to develop their potential to the highest possibilities.

BE AMAZING!
A 10-step guide to achieving your career goals.

Chapter 1: Assess your strengths and weaknesses.

Assessing your strengths and weaknesses is an essential step for personal and professional development.

Overview of the SWOT analysis framework and its benefits:

"SWOT" stands for: Strengths, Weakness, Opportunities and Threats.

A personal SWOT analysis is a self-assessment tool that helps individuals identify their strengths, weaknesses, opportunities, and threats. Here's a summary of each component of a personal SWOT analysis:

Strengths:

Strengths refer to your internal positive attributes or qualities that give you an advantage in achieving your goals. These are the areas where you excel and have a competitive edge over others. Identifying your strengths allows you to leverage them to maximize your personal growth and success.

Weaknesses:

Weaknesses are internal factors that hinder your progress or present challenges. These are areas where you may lack certain skills, experience limitations, or face personal shortcomings. Identifying weaknesses helps you recognize areas for improvement and take necessary steps to overcome them.

Opportunities:

Opportunities are external circumstances or factors that can contribute to your personal growth or success. These are favorable situations or possibilities that you can capitalize on to enhance your life or achieve your goals. Recognizing opportunities, enables you to align your actions and decisions to make the most of them.

Threats:

Threats are external factors that may pose risks, challenges, or obstacles to your personal well-being or goals. These can include trends, events, or circumstances that have the potential to impact your progress negatively. Identifying threats, helps you anticipate and prepare for potential risks, enabling you to navigate challenges effectively.

By conducting a personal SWOT analysis, you gain a comprehensive understanding of your strengths, weaknesses, opportunities, and threats. This self-assessment allows you to make informed decisions, set realistic goals, and develop strategies to maximize your strengths, address weaknesses, seize opportunities, and mitigate threats. It helps you focus on personal development, take advantage of favorable circumstances, and navigate potential challenges effectively.

Strengths

Definition and examples of strengths.

How to identify your strengths.

How to use your strengths to achieve your goals or overcome your challenges.

Identifying strengths is an important process that can help individuals understand their unique abilities and talents. Recognizing your strengths, allows you to leverage them effectively in various aspects of your life, such as career development, personal growth, and building relationships. Here are some steps to help you identify your strengths:

Self-reflection: Take some time for introspection and self-assessment. Consider your past experiences, achievements, and activities that have brought you joy and a sense of accomplishment. Reflect on tasks that come naturally to you or that you excel in.

Feedback from others: Seek feedback from people you trust, such as friends, family members, colleagues, or mentors. They may provide valuable insights about your strengths based on their observations of your abilities, skills, and character traits.

Personality assessments: Consider taking personality assessments or strengths-based assessments, such as the Myers-Briggs Type Indicator (MBTI), StrengthsFinder, or VIA Character Strengths. These assessments provide structured frameworks to help identify your unique strengths and personality traits.

Notice your energizing activities: Pay attention to activities that energize and motivate you. What tasks do you find engaging and enjoyable? Identifying these activities can reveal areas where your strengths lie.

Examples of strengths can vary from person to person, as everyone possesses a unique set of talents and abilities. Here are some examples of common strengths:

Leadership: The ability to guide and motivate others, make decisions, and take charge in a group or organizational setting.

Creativity: Generating innovative ideas, thinking outside the box, and finding unique solutions to problems.

Communication: Effective verbal and written communication skills, active listening, and the ability to articulate ideas clearly.

Problem-solving: Analytical thinking, identifying, and understanding complex problems, and developing practical solutions.

Adaptability: Being flexible and open to change, quickly adjusting to new situations, and finding opportunities within challenges.

Organization: Strong planning and time management skills, attention to detail, and the ability to prioritize tasks effectively.

Empathy: Understanding and relating to others' emotions and perspectives, showing compassion, and providing support.

Teamwork: Collaborating well with others, contributing ideas, and working effectively in a group setting.

Resilience: The ability to bounce back from setbacks, cope with adversity, and maintain a positive mindset.

Technical skills: Proficiency in specific areas such as coding, graphic design, data analysis, or any specialized skill related to your field.

Remember that these examples are not exhaustive, and each person may have a unique combination of strengths. The key is to identify and leverage your strengths in a way that aligns with your goals and aspirations.

Weaknesses

Definition and examples of weaknesses

How to identify your weaknesses

How to improve your weaknesses or compensate for them with your strengths

Identifying weaknesses, is equally important as recognizing strengths, as it allows individuals to understand areas for improvement and personal growth. Identifying weaknesses can lead to self-awareness and provide opportunities to develop new skills. Here are steps to help you identify your weaknesses:

Self-reflection: Reflect on tasks or activities that you find challenging or struggle with. Consider areas where you feel less confident or where you have received feedback for improvement.

Feedback from others: Seek honest feedback from people you trust, such as friends, family members, colleagues, or mentors. They can provide insights into areas where they believe you could improve or areas where they have noticed you facing challenges.

Assess your performance: Evaluate your performance in different areas of your life, such as work, academics, or personal relationships. Identify patterns where you may consistently encounter difficulties or struggle to achieve desired outcomes.

Personality assessments: Consider taking personality assessments or self-assessment tools that can shed light on your weaknesses. These assessments can provide insights into your personality traits, behavior patterns, and areas that may require further development.

Examples of weaknesses can vary from person to person, and it's important to approach them as areas for growth rather than limitations. Here are some common examples of weaknesses:

Procrastination: Delaying tasks or struggling with time management, leading to incomplete or rushed work.

Public speaking: Feeling nervous or uncomfortable when speaking in front of groups, making it challenging to convey ideas effectively.

Attention to detail: Struggling to notice small errors or inaccuracies, which can impact the quality of work.

Organization: Difficulty in maintaining an organized workspace or managing tasks efficiently, leading to missed deadlines or disorganized workflows.

Impatience: Feeling frustrated or restless when things don't progress as quickly as desired, potentially leading to impulsive decision-making.

Delegation: Struggling to delegate tasks and often taking on too much responsibility, which can lead to feeling overwhelmed or burned out.

Conflict resolution: Finding it challenging to navigate conflicts or disagreements, resulting in difficulty in finding mutually satisfactory resolutions.

Technical skills gaps: Lacking proficiency in certain technical skills or tools that are relevant to your field, which may limit your ability to perform certain tasks.

Perfectionism: Striving for perfection to an extent that it hampers progress or causes unnecessary stress and self-criticism.

Networking: Feeling uncomfortable or finding it difficult to connect with new people or build professional relationships, potentially limiting opportunities for collaboration or career growth.

Remember, these examples are not definitive and may vary based on individual circumstances. It's essential to approach weaknesses with a growth mindset, viewing them as areas for improvement rather than fixed limitations. By acknowledging weaknesses, individuals can take steps to develop skills, seek learning opportunities, or collaborate with others who possess complementary strengths.

Opportunities

Definition and examples of opportunities.

How to identify your opportunities.

How to leverage your opportunities with your strengths and skills.

Identifying personal opportunities involves recognizing circumstances or possibilities that can lead to personal growth, development, or achievement of your goals. Here are steps to help you identify your own opportunities:

Set clear goals: Start by defining your short-term and long-term goals. Having clarity about what you want to achieve allows you to identify opportunities that align with your aspirations.

Assess your passions and interests: Reflect on your passions, hobbies, and areas of genuine interest. Consider how you can explore or capitalize on these interests to create personal opportunities that bring fulfillment and joy.

Self-reflection and self-assessment: Take time for introspection and assess your strengths, skills, and talents. Identify areas where you excel or have a natural aptitude. These areas can present opportunities for personal growth and achievement.

Identify areas for improvement: Recognize your weaknesses or areas where you would like to enhance your skills or knowledge. By identifying these areas, you can seek opportunities for learning, training, or personal development to overcome these limitations.

Embrace challenges and step out of your comfort zone: Opportunities often arise from challenges or stepping out of your comfort zone. Be willing to take calculated risks, try new experiences, or explore unfamiliar territory. This mindset can lead to personal growth and open doors to unexpected opportunities.

Network and build relationships: Connect with individuals who share similar interests or goals. Engage in networking events, join professional or interest-based communities, and cultivate meaningful relationships. These connections can provide opportunities for collaboration, mentorship, or exposure to new possibilities.

Stay informed and seek knowledge: Keep yourself updated on current trends, industry developments, or relevant information related to your goals. Subscribe to newsletters, read books or articles, attend webinars or workshops, or enroll in courses that can expand your knowledge and expose you to potential opportunities.

Examples of personal opportunities can vary depending on your specific goals, interests, and circumstances. Here are some general examples:

Career advancement: Opportunities for promotions, leadership roles, or transitioning to a new career path aligned with your skills and aspirations.

Entrepreneurship: Starting your own business or pursuing a side venture based on your passions and expertise.

Education and learning opportunities: Pursuing higher education, acquiring certifications, or attending workshops and training programs to enhance your knowledge and skills.

Personal development: Opportunities for personal growth, such as improving communication skills, building resilience, or developing emotional intelligence.

Volunteer or community involvement: Engaging in volunteer work or community initiatives that align with your values, allowing you to contribute to causes you care about and expand your network.

Travel and cultural experiences: Exploring new places, immersing yourself in different cultures, and gaining a broader perspective on the world.

Health and wellness: Opportunities for improving physical and mental well-being, such as engaging in regular exercise, adopting healthy habits, or exploring mindfulness practices.

Creative pursuits: Opportunities for artistic expression, such as writing, painting, music, or other creative endeavors that bring fulfillment and personal satisfaction.

Remember that personal opportunities are unique to each individual and can be influenced by your specific goals, values, and passions. Regular self-reflection, staying open to new experiences, and being proactive in seeking growth and development can help you identify and seize personal opportunities that align with your aspirations.

Threats

Definition and examples of threats.

How to identify your threats.

How to minimize your threats with your strengths and skills.

Identifying personal threats involves recognizing potential challenges, risks, or obstacles that may hinder your personal well-being, goals, or aspirations. By identifying threats, you can take proactive measures to mitigate or overcome them. Here are steps to help you identify personal threats:

Self-reflection: Take time for self-reflection and introspection. Consider factors that may pose challenges or risks to your personal well-being or goals. Reflect on your fears, limitations, or areas where you have faced difficulties in the past.

Assess external factors: Evaluate external circumstances or situations that may pose threats to your personal life or goals. Consider social, economic, or environmental factors that can impact your well-being or create obstacles.

Conduct a SWOT analysis: Perform a personal SWOT (Strengths, Weaknesses, Opportunities, and Threats) analysis. Identify threats that may arise from both internal and external factors, such as personal limitations, negative influences, or external challenges.

Seek feedback: Engage in conversations with trusted friends, family members, mentors, or advisors. Seek their honest feedback on areas where they perceive threats to your personal growth or well-being. Their perspectives can provide valuable insights that you may not have considered.

Stay informed: Keep yourself informed about current events, trends, or developments that may have an impact on your personal life or goals. This awareness can help you identify potential threats in areas such as finances, health, relationships, or career.

Examples of personal threats can vary based on individual circumstances. Here are some general examples:

Financial instability: Facing financial challenges, such as job loss, debt, or unexpected expenses, that can impact your ability to meet your financial obligations or pursue your goals.

Health issues: Dealing with physical or mental health concerns that can hinder your overall well-being or limit your ability to achieve your personal aspirations.

Negative influences: Surrounding yourself with negative or toxic relationships, environments, or influences that can undermine your self-esteem, confidence, or progress toward your goals.

Lack of support: Not having a supportive network of family, friends, or mentors who can provide guidance, encouragement, or assistance when needed.

Personal limitations: Recognizing personal weaknesses or limitations that can hinder your personal growth, such as poor time management, lack of assertiveness, or difficulty in adapting to change.

Lack of opportunities: Facing limited access to opportunities, resources, or networks that can impede your progress or hinder your ability to achieve your goals.

Changing circumstances: Unforeseen events or circumstances, such as natural disasters, political instability, or economic downturns, that can disrupt your personal life or plans.

Negative self-talk: Engaging in negative self-talk or self-doubt that undermines your confidence, motivation, or belief in your abilities.

Lack of work-life balance: Struggling to maintain a healthy balance between work, personal life, and self-care, leading to burnout or neglecting important aspects of your life.

Fear of failure: Allowing fear of failure to hold you back from taking risks or pursuing opportunities, limiting your personal growth and potential.

Remember, personal threats are not meant to discourage you but rather to create awareness. By identifying potential threats, you can develop strategies, seek support, or make proactive decisions to overcome or mitigate them. Focus on building resilience, developing coping mechanisms, and seeking opportunities to turn threats into opportunities for personal growth and transformation.

Conclusion-

To assess your strengths, think about what you are good at, what you enjoy doing, what others compliment you on, and what makes you stand out from others.

To assess your weaknesses, think about what you struggle with, what you avoid doing, what others criticize you on, and what holds you back from achieving your goals.

To assess your opportunities, think about the current and future trends, demands, and needs in your field or industry, and how you can take advantage of them with your strengths and skills.

To assess your threats, think about the potential risks, challenges, and obstacles that you may face in your field or industry, and how you can overcome them with your strengths and skills.

Chapter 2: Define your vision and mission.

Defining your vision and mission is an important step for personal and professional development. It helps you to clarify your purpose, direction, and goals, here are some steps to define your vision and mission:

Identify your strengths and weaknesses. Think about what you are good at, what you enjoy doing, what others compliment you on, and what makes you stand out from others. Also think about what you struggle with, what you avoid doing, what others criticize you for, and what holds you back from achieving your goals.

Determine your organization's purpose. Think about why you choose to exist together, beyond financial gain. What do you believe in? What problem are you trying to solve? What impact do you want to have on the world?

Visualize where your business will be in five to 10 years. Think about the difference you'll create in your customers' lives or the larger world when you ultimately realize your purpose. What will you achieve? How will you grow? How will you measure your success?

Shape your statement. Write a clear and concise statement that summarizes your vision and mission. Use positive and inspiring language that reflects your values and culture. Make sure your statement is realistic and achievable, but also ambitious and challenging.

Here are some examples of vision and mission statements from well-known companies:

Sweetgreen: Vision: To inspire healthier communities by connecting people to real food. Mission: To make healthy food accessible and affordable for everyone.

Nike: Vision: To bring inspiration and innovation to every athlete in the world. If you have a body, you are an athlete. Mission: To be the most innovative and sustainable sports brand in the world.

Etsy: Vision: To keep commerce human. Mission: To empower creative entrepreneurs to sell their goods online.

Chapter 3: Set SMART goals and action plans.

Setting SMART goals and action plans is a useful way to achieve your objectives and measure your progress, here are some steps to set SMART goals and action plans:

Set SMART goals.

SMART stands for: Specific, Measurable, Achievable, Relevant, and Time-bound.

A SMART goal answers the questions: What do I want to accomplish? Why is this goal important? Who is involved? How will I measure my success? When will I achieve it?

Create a list of actions. Next, create a list of tasks you need to complete to reach your goal. This process helps you break down your goal into manageable steps and prioritize them. For each task, assign a deadline, a responsible person, and a status (such as not started, in progress, or completed).

Set a timeline. A timeline helps you visualize your goal and track your progress. You can use a calendar, a spreadsheet, or a project management tool to create your timeline. Include your start date, end date, milestones, and deadlines for each task. Update your timeline regularly as you complete your tasks or encounter changes.

Identify potential risks and challenges. No goal is without obstacles or uncertainties. It's important to anticipate and prepare for any potential risks and challenges that might affect your goal or action plan. For each risk or challenge, identify the likelihood, impact, and mitigation strategy.

Review and adjust your plan. Finally, review your plan regularly and adjust as needed. Check if you are on track with your timeline and budget, if you are meeting your milestones and deadlines, and if you are achieving your desired outcomes. Celebrate your successes and learn from your failures.

I recommend creating a status traffic light: Red- Not started, Yellow- In progress, Green- Completed.

Executive meetings focus on the reds first, then the yellows, and don't forget to celebrate completed accomplishments and give credit where credit is due.

Here is an example of a SMART goal and action plan:

SMART goal: Increase the number of monthly users of Techfirm's mobile app by 20% by June 30th, 2023, by optimizing our app-store listing and creating targeted social media campaigns.

Action plan:

Task 1: Conduct keyword research and optimize app-store listing with relevant keywords and descriptions. Deadline: January 31st, 2023. Responsible: Jane (product manager). Status: In progress.

Task 2: Design and launch social media campaigns on Facebook, Instagram, and Twitter to promote the app's features and benefits. Deadline: March 31st, 2023. Responsible: Mark (marketing manager). Status: Not started.

Task 3: Monitor and analyze app-store analytics and social media metrics to measure user acquisition and retention rates. Deadline: Ongoing. Responsible: Lisa (data analyst). Status: Not started.

Timeline: *"See attached spreadsheet for details".*

Risks and challenges:

Risk 1: Low app-store ranking due to high competition. Likelihood: High. Impact: High. Mitigation: Use SEO best practices and user feedback to improve app-store listing.

Risk 2: Low social media engagement due to low brand awareness. Likelihood: Medium. Impact: Medium. Mitigation: Use paid ads and influencer marketing to boost social media reach and engagement.

Review and adjustment: Review the action plan monthly and update the timeline, status, and metrics accordingly.

Here are some examples of SMART goals for different areas of life:

Personal SMART goal: I want to read 12 books this year to improve my knowledge and vocabulary. I will read one book per month and track my progress on Goodreads. This goal is achievable because I enjoy reading and have access to many books. This goal is relevant because reading can enrich my mind and expand my horizons.

Business SMART goal: I want to increase the revenue of my online store by 20% in the next quarter. I will do this by optimizing my website, running paid ads, and creating email campaigns. This goal is measurable because I can track the sales and conversions on my website. This goal is relevant because increasing revenue can help me grow my business and reach more customers.

Work SMART goal: I want to improve my presentation skills and deliver a successful pitch to a potential client next month. I will do this by taking an online course on presentation skills, practicing with my colleagues, and getting feedback. This goal is achievable because I have the time and resources to learn and practice. This goal is relevant because presentation skills are important for my career and can help me win more projects.

Leadership SMART goal: I want to develop a more cohesive and productive team by the end of the year. I will do this by conducting regular team meetings, providing constructive feedback, and recognizing achievements. This goal is measurable because I can monitor the team's performance and satisfaction. This goal is relevant because a strong team can improve the quality and efficiency of our work.

Remember that SMART goals can help you to achieve your dreams by making them more concrete and actionable.

Chapter 4: Build your network and mentorship.

How to build your network and mentorship. here are some steps you can take:

Establish trust and rapport with your mentor and contacts by being respectful, punctual, prepared, honest, and appreciative.

Ask for introductions and referrals from people who can help you advance your career. Be clear about your purpose and value proposition and follow up with a thank-you note.

Seek feedback and guidance on your work, skills, and career path. Be specific about what you want to learn or improve, remain open to constructive criticism and suggestions, and apply your learnings.

Learn from their stories and experiences that can inspire and motivate you, as well as teach you valuable lessons.

Leverage networking and mentoring for growth by maintaining contact with your mentor and contacts, sharing useful information, providing feedback, expressing appreciation, and seeking new opportunities.

Here a few real examples of people who created their network and mentorship, here are some examples:

Steve Jobs mentoring Mark Zuckerberg. The two tech giants are said to have taken walks around Palo Alto discussing how Zuckerberg might manage and develop Facebook, as well as entrepreneurship.

Maya Angelou mentoring Oprah Winfrey. The renowned poet and author was a mentor and a friend to Oprah, guiding her through some of the most important years of her life.

Christian Dior mentoring Yves Saint-Laurent. The two fashion designers worked together at Dior's haute couture house, where Saint-Laurent learned the secrets of the trade and how to run a company.

Warren Buffett mentoring Bill Gates. The two billionaires have a long-standing friendship and mutual admiration, with Gates turning to Buffett for advice on various subjects and referring to him as a one-of-a-kind.

Randstad's leadership development mentoring program. The global staffing and recruitment company has a program that pairs high-potential employees with senior leaders for a year-long mentoring relationship, focusing on career development, networking, and leadership skills.

These are just some of the many examples of successful network and mentorship creation. I hope they inspire you to find your own mentors and contacts.

Chapter 5: Learn new skills and update your knowledge.

To learn new skills and update your knowledge, here are some tips you can follow:

Create a schedule with fixed study times. Creating structure for your study plan makes it much quicker and easier to acquire and master new skills.

Get feedback. Feedback is crucial for improving your performance, identifying your strengths and weaknesses, and learning from your mistakes.

Start with core skills. Core skills are the fundamental skills that are essential for your field or industry. They provide a solid foundation for learning more advanced or specialized skills.

Take things step by step. Breaking down complex skills into smaller and manageable chunks can help you learn faster and more effectively. You can also use the SMART (Specific, Measurable, Achievable, Relevant, Time-bound) framework to set realistic and attainable goals for each step.

Learn from other people's experience. You can learn a lot from observing and interacting with people who have the skills and knowledge you want to acquire. You can also read books, articles, blogs, podcasts, or watch videos that share valuable insights and tips.

Learn from experts. Experts are people who have mastered the skills and knowledge you want to learn. They can provide you with expert guidance, advice, and feedback that can accelerate your learning process.

Find a mentor. A mentor is someone who has the experience, knowledge, and connections that you aspire to have. A mentor can help you with career development, networking, and personal growth.

Set realistic goals. Setting realistic goals can help you stay motivated, focused, and accountable for your learning progress. You can use the SMART framework to set goals that are specific, measurable, achievable, relevant, and time bound.

Basic coding. Coding is the skill of assigning a computer a task to do based on the guidelines you've outlined. Coding is becoming increasingly important in many workplaces, as it allows you to create websites, apps, software, or automate tasks.

Data analysis and statistics. Data analysis and statistics are the skills of collecting, organizing, interpreting, and presenting data to draw conclusions and make decisions. Data analysis and statistics are essential for many fields and industries, as they help you understand trends, patterns, problems, and opportunities.

Digital literacy. Digital literacy is the skill of using technology effectively and efficiently for various purposes. Digital literacy includes being able to use different devices, software, platforms, tools, and applications for communication, collaboration, research, problem-solving, creativity, and productivity.

Foreign language. Foreign language is the skill of communicating in a language other than your native one. Foreign languages can help you expand your career opportunities, connect with different cultures, access more information sources, and enhance your cognitive abilities.

Project management. Project management is the skill of planning, organizing, leading, and controlling projects from start to finish. Project management includes defining the project scope, objectives, deliverables, resources, budget, timeline, risks, and stakeholders; managing the project team; monitoring and reporting on the project progress; and ensuring the project quality and satisfaction.

Now, check these real examples of people who learned new skills and updated their knowledge:

Jessica Lau, a writer at Zapier, shares how she learned a new language, learned how to knit, and even became skilled at writing with her non-dominant hand at the age of 30-something. She used seven strategies to boost her expertise, such as setting clear goals, adopting a growth mindset, using active learning strategies, using different learning mediums, learning from someone with more experience, practicing, and taking frequent breaks.

David DeSteno, a psychologist, and author of the book "Emotional Success: The Power of Gratitude, Compassion, and Pride", shares how he learned new skills by using prosocial emotions. He explains how these emotions, such as gratitude, compassion, and pride, can help people overcome challenges, build resilience, and achieve their goals. He also shares how he learned from his own research and experiments on how emotions affect behavior.

Zapier's Talent Acquisition team, a group of recruiters and hiring managers at Zapier, shares how they learned new skills and updated their knowledge by participating in Zapier's secondment program. This program allows employees to temporarily work in different departments and roles within the company. The team members were able to leverage their existing skills and experiences to add value to other business-critical departments, such as Customer Support and Marketing. They also learned new skills and tools that helped them grow professionally and personally.

Amy Edmondson, a professor at Harvard Business School and author of the book "The Fearless Organization: Creating Psychological Safety in the Workplace for Learning, Innovation, and Growth", shares how she learned new skills and updated her knowledge by helping her employees learn from each other. She explains how she created a culture of psychological safety in her workplace, where people feel comfortable sharing ideas, asking questions, and giving feedback. She also explains how she used the "Learning Loop" model to facilitate effective peer learning among her employees.

These are some examples of people who learned new skills and updated their knowledge.

Remember that learning new skills is not only a way to enhance your career and adapt to change, but also a way to keep your brain healthy and happy.

Chapter 6: Showcase your value and achievements.

How to showcase your value and achievements, here are some tips you can follow:

Know your goals and expectations. Before you start showcasing your value and achievements, you need to understand what your manager, clients, or potential employers expect from you and what your goals are. This will help you align your message and focus on the most relevant and impactful aspects of your work.

Use the STAR method. One of the most effective ways to showcase your value and achievements is to use the STAR method. STAR stands for Situation, Task, Action, Result. It is a framework that helps you structure your stories and provide context, actions, and outcomes. For example, you can say "I was assigned to lead a project with a tight deadline and a limited budget (Situation). My task was to deliver a high-quality product that met the client's specifications (Task). I coordinated the project team, delegated tasks, managed risks, and communicated with stakeholders (Action). As a result, we completed the project on time, within budget, and exceeded the client's expectations (Result)".

Be honest and balanced. When showcasing your value and achievements, you need to be honest and balanced. Avoid exaggerating or lying about your work and results, as this can damage your credibility and reputation. Instead, use facts, data, and evidence to support your claims and achievements. Also, acknowledge your challenges, mistakes, and areas of improvement, and show how you learned from them or overcame them.

Use positive language. The way you showcase your value and achievements can affect how your audience perceives you and your work. Therefore, you need to use positive and confident language that reflects your professionalism and enthusiasm. Avoid words that diminish or undermine your value or achievements, such as "just", "only", "a little", or "sorry". Instead, use words that emphasize or reinforce your value or achievements, such as "successfully", "effectively", "significantly", or "proudly". You can also use active voice, strong verbs, and adjectives to make your message more powerful and engaging.

Create a portfolio of your work. One of the best ways to showcase your value and achievements to potential employers is to create a portfolio of your work. This can include projects, products, or services that you have contributed to or led, as well as any awards, recognitions, or testimonials that you have received. A portfolio can help you demonstrate your skills, creativity, and impact in a visual and tangible way. You can create a portfolio online using platforms like LinkedIn, Behance, GitHub, or WordPress.

Track and document your results. Another way to showcase your value and achievements is to track and document your results. Use metrics, data, and evidence to quantify and qualify your impact and contribution. For example, you can use tools like Google Analytics, Excel, or Trello to measure and report on your website traffic, sales, productivity, or project completion. Tracking and documenting your results can help you monitor your performance, identify areas of improvement, and communicate your value and achievements with data and facts.

I hope this helps you showcase your value and achievements.

Chapter 7: Seek feedback and improve yourself.

How to seek feedback and improve yourself. Here are some tips and strategies:

Start with thank you. When someone gives you feedback, express your gratitude, and avoid getting defensive or explaining yourself. This shows that you appreciate their input and are willing to listen.

Restate what you heard. To check your understanding and make the other person feel heard, repeat back what they said in your own words. For example, "What I hear you saying is that I need to work on my presentation skills."

Ask for feedback in real time. Don't wait until your annual review or a formal meeting to ask for feedback. Seek it out regularly and informally, right after you complete a task or project. For example, "How do you think I did in that meeting? What could I have done better?"

Pose specific questions. Don't ask vague or general questions like "Do you have any feedback for me?" Instead, ask focused and open-ended questions that elicit specific and actionable responses. For example, "What are some strengths and weaknesses of my report? How can I improve my writing style?"

Listen actively and attentively. When receiving feedback, pay attention to what the other person is saying and show interest and curiosity. Don't interrupt or jump to conclusions. Ask clarifying questions if needed and take notes if possible.

Use feedback to improve performance. Feedback is only useful if you act on it and apply it to your work. Identify the key points and suggestions from the feedback and plan to implement them. Track your progress and seek more feedback to see if you are improving.

Chapter 8: Embrace challenges and opportunities.

To embrace challenges and opportunities, here are some tips and strategies:

Adjust your mindset. Instead of seeing challenges as threats or obstacles, see them as opportunities to learn, grow, and improve. Adopt a growth mindset that believes you can develop your abilities and potential through effort and feedback. For example, you can say: *"I can do this"* or *"This is a chance to show what I can do"*.

Seek feedback. Feedback is a valuable source of information that can help you identify your strengths and weaknesses and guide your actions and decisions. Seek feedback regularly from your manager, colleagues, clients, or anyone else who can offer you useful insights. For example, you can ask: *"How can I improve my performance?"* or *"What did I do well in this project?"*.

Act. Challenges require you to act and overcome them. Don't avoid or procrastinate on them but face them head-on with confidence and courage. Take small steps, break down big goals into manageable tasks, and celebrate your progress. For example, you can say: *"I will start working on this today"* or *"I have completed this part of the challenge"*.

Here are some inspiring stories from people who embraced challenges and opportunities:

J.K. Rowling. The author of the Harry Potter series faced many hardships before achieving fame and fortune. She was a single mother living on welfare, suffering from depression, and rejected by 12 publishers. She persevered and continued to write, eventually finding a publisher who gave her a chance. Her books became a global phenomenon and made her one of the richest and most influential women in the world.

Steve Jobs. The co-founder of Apple was a college dropout who was fired from his own company at the age of 30. He faced several failures and setbacks in his career, such as the commercial flop of the NeXT computer and the diagnosis of pancreatic cancer. He bounced back and returned to Apple, leading the company to create innovative products such as the iPod, iPhone, and iPad. He is widely regarded as one of the most visionary and influential leaders in the tech industry.

Malala Yousafzai. The Pakistani activist for girls' education was shot in the head by the Taliban when she was 15 years old for speaking out against their oppression. She survived and became a global symbol of courage and resilience. She continued to advocate for girls' rights and education, winning the Nobel Peace Prize in 2014. She is also the youngest-ever UN Messenger of Peace and the founder of the Malala Fund, a non-profit organization that supports girls' education around the world.

Chapter 9: Balance your work and life.

To balance your work and life, here are some tips and strategies:

Identify your priorities. Work-life balance is about aligning your actions with your values and goals. You need to decide what is important, essential, and non-negotiable for you in both your work and personal life. Then, you need to allocate your time and energy accordingly1. For example, you can say "My family is my top priority" or "I want to advance in my career".

Schedule your time. A key aspect of work-life balance is managing your time effectively. You need to plan, set boundaries, and stick to them. You also need to make time for the activities and relationships that enrich your life. For example, you can say: *"I will work from 9 a.m. to 5 p.m."* or *"I will spend an hour every day on my hobby"*.

Find enjoyment at work. Work-life balance is not only about reducing stress and avoiding burnout, but also about finding meaning and satisfaction in your work. You need to focus on the positive aspects of your job, such as the impact you make, the skills you learn, or the people you work with. For example, you can say: *"I love helping my clients solve their problems"* or *"I enjoy working with my team"*.

Have a life outside of work. Work-life balance is also about having a rich and diverse personal life that fulfills you and makes you happy. You need to pursue your interests, hobbies, passions, and relationships outside of your work. For example, you can say: *"I like to read books"* or *"I have a close group of friends"*.

Here some real examples of people who balanced their work and life:

Mark Zuckerberg, the co-founder, and CEO of Facebook took two months of paternity leave when his daughters were born.

Sheryl Sandberg, the COO of Facebook, leaves the office at 5:30 p.m. every day to have dinner with her kids.

Reed Hastings, the CEO of Netflix, takes six weeks of vacation every year and encourages his employees to do the same.

Susan Wojcicki, the CEO of YouTube, also gets home by 6 p.m. every night to have dinner with her five children.

A stay-at-home parent who tackles work assignments while their newborn is napping.

A student who prioritizes spending time with their friends rather than rushing ahead to study for an upcoming midterm exam.

A lawyer who consciously unplugs when on vacation.

A new employee who dedicates extra time to tasks and responsibilities.

A manager who establishes communications boundaries and won't respond to emails after 6 p.m.

An employee who crafts their schedule to work specific days so that they can take care of their elderly parents.

These are some examples of how people balance their work and life according to their own priorities and preferences.

There is no one right way to achieve work-life balance or work-life integration, as it depends on your personal and professional goals and responsibilities.

Chapter 10: Celebrate your success and keep growing.

To celebrate your success and keep growing, here are some tips:

Reflect on your wins. After achieving a goal or completing a big task, always take time to reflect on what you've accomplished. Consider the variables of your efforts that were successful and take inventory of what you learned. Use this reflection time to consider what you'd do the same or differently next time.

Express gratitude. When you're in the middle of the most difficult stretches of working toward a goal, gratitude helps you maintain perspective. It also allows you to honor your hard work after completing a task. Practice gratitude for your success by making a list of what you're grateful for regarding the task. List out what made your success possible, reflect on your hard work, and give credit to others who helped you. Show gratitude to those who supported you in your journey by giving them small gifts or handwritten notes.

Organize an activity. Plan an outing with friends or coworkers to celebrate successful milestones. Organize a celebratory dinner with friends, a team-building activity, an awards ceremony, or a self-care night with loved ones.

Practice self-care. A great way to celebrate success is to take time for self-love. Exercise, meditate, call a friend, or make your favorite meal. Accomplishing a goal takes lots of hard work, and taking time to unwind is a healthy way to replenish your intrinsic motivation levels before setting your next goal.

Celebrate with music and movement. Next time you achieve a goal, put on your favorite song and dance. Strike a power pose. Do some yoga or take a walk outside. Use your happiness to both celebrate success and elevate your mood.

Celebrate with your supporters. Celebrate success by including your supporters. Go out for a nice dinner. Give small gifts of appreciation. Tell them how much they mean to you. The secret to living is giving, even when you're celebrating your own accomplishments.

Celebrate fairly and appropriately. When you celebrate achievement in the right way, you'll likely increase confidence and motivation, leading to happier and more productive teams. If you rarely acknowledge a job well done (or celebrate in a way that feels forced, unfair or inappropriate) there's a risk that morale and dedication will slip away. Make sure your celebration is meaningful, sincere, and proportional to the achievement.

Remember that celebrating success is an important part of building and maintaining an effective, self-assured team, boosting your own confidence, and making your organization a great place to work.

Examples of how people celebrated their success and keep growing:

Whitney Johnson, the author of the book "Smart Growth", shares how she and her team at Disruption Advisors celebrate their achievements by using the S Curve of Learning model. They celebrate early and small wins at the launch point of the curve, express gratitude and organize activities at the sweet spot of the curve, and practice self-care and celebrate with their supporters at the mastery point of the curve. They also celebrate fairly and appropriately according to the magnitude and impact of their achievements.

Oprah Winfrey, the media mogul, and philanthropist, celebrates her success by giving back to others. She has donated millions of dollars to various causes, such as education, women's empowerment, and disaster relief. She also hosts an annual event called "Oprah's Favorite Things", where she surprises her audience members with gifts that she personally loves.

Elon Musk, the founder and CEO of Tesla and SpaceX, celebrates his success by setting new and bigger goals. He has a vision of making humanity a multi-planetary species and has launched several ambitious projects, such as Starlink, Neuralink, and Hyperloop. He also celebrates with music and movement, as he once danced on stage at a Tesla event in China.

J.K. Rowling, the author of the Harry Potter series, celebrates her success by reflecting on her wins and overcoming her challenges. She has faced many hardships in her life, such as poverty, depression, and rejection. She used her imagination and creativity to write stories that inspired millions of people around the world. She also celebrates by expressing gratitude to her fans and supporters.

Michael Jordan, the basketball legend, and entrepreneur, celebrates his success by practicing self-care and celebrating with his team. He has won six NBA championships and numerous awards in his career. He also faced many failures and setbacks, such as being cut from his high school basketball team and losing his father to murder. He used his failures as motivation to work harder and improve his skills. He also celebrates by enjoying his hobbies, such as golfing and fishing.

Remember that celebrating your success is not only a reward for your hard work, but also a way to boost your confidence, motivation, and happiness.

Now that you know the ten steps, work on each one, create and follow your own treasure map and **BE AMAZING!**

"Life is a constant awaking… closer to your dreams!"